W9-BEU-147

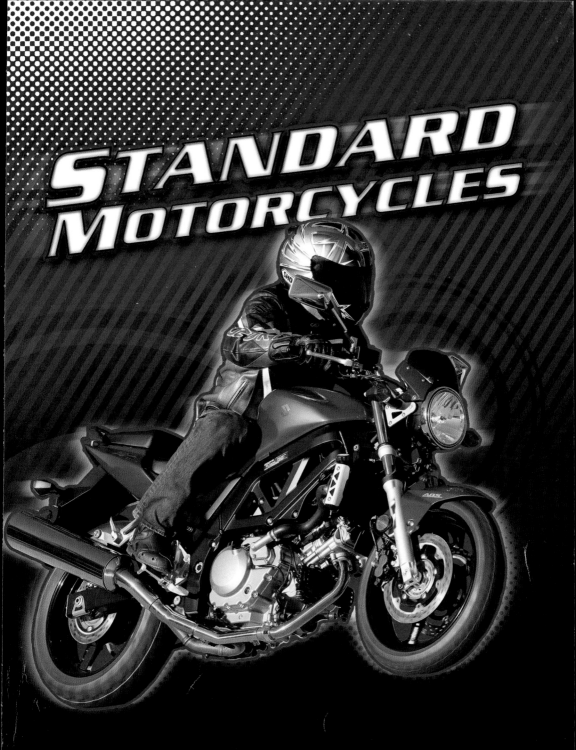

STANDARD MOTORCYCLES

BY THOMAS STREISSGUTH

BELLWETHER MEDIA · MINNEAPOLIS, MN

Are you ready to take it to the extreme?
Torque books thrust you into the action-packed
world of sports, vehicles, and adventure. These books
may include dirt, smoke, fire, and dangerous stunts.
WARNING: Read at your own risk.

Library of Congress Cataloging-in-Publication Data

Streissguth, Thomas, 1958–
  Standard motorcycles / by Thomas Streissguth.
    p. cm. – (Torque–motorcycles)
  Summary: "Full color photography accompanies engaging information about Standard
Motorcycles. The combination of high-interest subject matter and light text is intended for
students in grades 3 through 7"–Provided by publisher.
  Includes bibliographical references and index.
  ISBN-13: 978–1–60014–159–1 (hardcover : alk. paper)
  ISBN-10: 1–60014–159–5 (hardcover : alk. paper)
  1. Motorcycles–Juvenile literature. I. Title.

TL440.15.S77 2008
629.227'5–dc22   2007040749

This edition first published in 2008 by Bellwether Media.

CONTENTS

WHAT IS A STANDARD MOTORCYCLE?

You can see them speeding down the open highway and winding through city traffic. Standard motorcycles are all-purpose street bikes.

Motorcycles come in many different styles. Most styles are specialized for a particular type of riding. **Cruisers** are comfortable bikes built for long-distance riding. **Sport bikes** are built for acceleration, handling, and high-speed performance.

7

FAST FACT

MOTORCYCLE RIDERS SHOULD TAKE A TRAINING COURSE TO LEARN HOW TO OPERATE THEIR BIKES SAFELY. SOME STATES REQUIRE A PERSON TO TAKE A MOTORCYCLE TRAINING COURSE BEFORE THEY ARE ALLOWED TO OPERATE A BIKE.

Choppers are fancy custom-made bikes that are mostly for show. Standard bikes are the most basic style. They are great for all kinds of street riding. They usually have the fewest **accessories**. Some people even call them "naked bikes."

FEATURES

Most standard motorcycle engines have two fuel-burning **cylinders**. Some have as many as six cylinders. Engine size is measured in cubic centimeters (cc). Standard motorcycle engines can range anywhere from 50cc to more than 1000cc. A bigger engine gives more power. It also burns fuel faster. Standard motorcycles with big engines are often called "muscle bikes."

The operation of a standard motorcycle is simple. The **transmission** has five or six speeds. The rider changes speeds with a **clutch** lever on the handlebars and a gearshift under the left foot. **Disc brakes** are standard equipment. A **suspension system** cushions the ride.

The "look" of a standard motorcycle gives it away. The rider sits upright in his seat. His feet rest on foot pegs directly beneath him. This is different from the rider position on other motorcycles. Riders on sport bikes lean forward to reduce wind resistance. Riders on choppers and cruisers lean back in their seats for more comfort.

Good riders always keep safety in mind. They wear helmets for protection. A crash on a motorcycle moving at full speed can be deadly. Goggles and gloves are often worn for added safety.

FAST FACT

THE MOST POPULAR AMERICAN MOTORCYCLE IS HARLEY-DAVIDSON. HARLEYS HAVE BEEN AROUND FOR OVER ONE HUNDRED YEARS.

STANDARD MOTORCYCLES IN ACTION

Someone may own a standard motorcycle for many reasons. It usually costs less than other motorcycles. Its basic design makes it easy to manage. A motorcycle can go anywhere a car can go. Some riders use standard motorcycles just to get around town. Riders like standard motorcycles because they use less fuel than cars. Owners save money when a vehicle uses less fuel.

FAST FACT

MOTORCYCLISTS LOVE TO GATHER AT HUGE RALLIES. ONE OF THE MOST POPULAR RALLIES TAKES PLACE IN STURGIS, SOUTH DAKOTA. THOUSANDS OF MOTORCYCLES LINE THE CROWDED STREETS FOR SEVERAL DAYS EVERY SUMMER.

Motorcycles are also fun for cross-country rides or camping trips. Long-distance riders can pack their gear into **saddlebags**. Some bikes have seats long enough for a passenger to ride behind the driver.

Some people think that motorcycles are the most exciting way to travel. Riding a motorcycle is a great way to experience freedom, fun, and the open road.

FAST FACT

STANDARD MOTORCYCLES ARE VERY POPULAR IN EUROPE.

GLOSSARY

accessories–extra items added as decoration or to make something more useful

chopper–a customized motorcycle; choppers are changed to suit a rider's tastes.

clutch–a lever that allows the rider to change engine gears

cruiser–a motorcycle built for relaxed riding

cylinder–a hollow chamber inside an engine in which fuel is burned to create power

disc brake–a mechanism that slows and stops the wheels with a round, flat metal disc

saddlebags–deep leather bags placed on both sides of the rear wheel and used to carry supplies

sport bike–a style of motorcycle built for maximum acceleration, handling, and speed

suspension system–a series of springs and shock absorbers that connect the body of a vehicle to its wheels

transmission–the part of an engine that sends power to the wheels

TO LEARN MORE

AT THE LIBRARY

David, Jack. *Choppers*. Minneapolis, Minn.: Bellwether, 2008.

David, Jack. *Cruisers*. Minneapolis, Minn.: Bellwether, 2008.

Dayton, Connor. *Street Bikes*. New York: PowerKids Press, 2007.

Sherman, Josepha. *The Story of Harley-Davidson*. Hockessin, Del.: Mitchell Lane, 2005.

ON THE WEB

Learning more about motorcycles is as easy as 1, 2, 3.

1. Go to www.factsurfer.com

2. Enter "motorcycles" into search box.

3. Click the "Surf" button and you will see a list of related web sites.

With factsurfer.com, finding more information is just a click away.

INDEX

The images in this book are reproduced through the courtesy of:
American Suzuki Motor Corporation, front cover; Moto Guzzi, pp.
5, 15, 18, 19, 21; Luís Louro, p. 6; Yamaha Motor Corporation, pp. 7, 9;
Piaggio USA, Inc., pp. 8, 13, 17; American Honda Motor Co., Inc., pp.
11, 12.